Contents

C000174196

2	Place value	**26**	Capacity
4	More place value	**28**	Money
6	Rounding and negative numbers	**30**	Time
8	Addition	**32**	Angles
10	Subtraction	**34**	2D shapes
12	Factors and multiples	**36**	Symmetry
14	Multiplication	**38**	Co-ordinates and translations
16	Division	**40**	Statistics
18	Fractions	**42**	Quick test
20	Decimals	**44**	Explorer's logbook
22	Length	**46**	Answers
24	Weight		

Introduction

If you are wild about learning and wild about animals – this book is for you! It will take you on a wild adventure, where you will practise key maths skills and explore the amazing world of animals along the way.

Each maths topic is introduced in a clear and simple way with lots of interesting activities to complete so that you can practise what you have learned.

You should attempt the tasks without a calculator unless instructed otherwise, but calculators may be used to check your answers.

Alongside every topic you will uncover fascinating facts about minibeasts. A minibeast is a small animal or 'creepy crawly' that can be found on land and in water.

When you have completed each topic, record the animals that you have seen and the skills that you have learned in the explorer's logbook on pages 44–45.

Good luck, explorer!

Pamela Wild

Place value

FACT FILE

Animal: Centipede
Habitat: Often moist habitats under rocks, logs and leaves
Size: 2 to 3 cm long
Lifespan: Up to 5 years (if it can avoid predators!)
Diet: Woodlice, worms, slugs and spiders

Our **number system** is amazing and very simple to understand because it is based on sets of 10. We only have nine symbols for our numbers – 1,2,3,4,5,6,7,8,9 – we also use 0, which is very useful for holding a digit's place in the columns. Every number is made up of these digits and zero! Discover how good you are at reading, writing, ordering and comparing numbers in the first four columns:

Th (thousands)   H (hundreds)   T (tens)   U (units)

Task 1	Write down the value of the underlined digit.

a 590<u>3</u> _____   b 4<u>6</u>24 _____

c 30<u>7</u>8 _____   d <u>8</u>150 _____

Task 2	Write these numbers in words.

a 7009 _____

b 2980 _____

c 1206 _____

Write these numbers in figures.

d three thousand four hundred and twenty _____

e four thousand and four _____

f eight thousand and thirty _____

Task 3 Compare these numbers by inserting < (is less than) or > (is greater than) in the box.

a 7899 ☐ 7989   **b** 3072 ☐ 3027   **c** 1489 ☐ 1894

Put these numbers in order of size, starting with the biggest.

d 1012   1201   1102   1112   1221   2121

_____

e 5554   5445   5545   5050   5454   5504

_____

WILD FACT

Centipedes have flattened heads with two long antennae. The antennae detect prey – soft-bodied creatures like a spider or earthworm.

Task 4 Write the number which is **1000** more than:

a 6709 _____   **b** 5061 _____   **c** 990 _____

Write the number which is **1000** less than:

d 4862 _____   **e** 8091 _____   **f** 1845 _____

WILD FACT

The name 'centipede' means '100 feet', but in fact a centipede can have between 15 and 177 pairs of legs, depending on the species.

Exploring Further ...

Fill in the numbers on the centipede's legs.

Start Here
6201
+10   −10
+100   −100
+300   −300
+1000   −1000
6044
Start Here

Now creep to pages **44–45** to record what you have learned in your explorer's logbook.

More place value

To understand our number system fully, you have to understand the columns. Each column is ten times bigger or smaller than the column next to it.

Th	H	T	U
			1
		1	0
	1	0	0
1	0	0	0

A 1 in the tens column is ten times bigger than a 1 in the units column. It is ten times smaller than a 1 in the hundreds column, and it is 100 times smaller than a 1 in the thousands column

The Romans' number system was very complicated in comparison. They had three different symbols for one, ten and a hundred:

I = 1 unit, X = 1 ten, C = 1 hundred

Here are some more of their symbols. Can you see the patterns?

I = 1	II = 2	III = 3	IV = 4	V = 5	VI = 6	VII = 7
VIII = 8	IX = 9	X = 10	XI = 11	XX = 20	L = 50	C = 100

Task 1   Make each of these numbers 10 times bigger.

a T U	b H T U	c Th H T U	d Th H T U	e Th H T U
5	9 2	6 8 1	4 0 5	7 9 0
____	____	____	____	____

Task 2
Make each of these numbers 10 times smaller.

a T U	b H T U	c Th H T U	d Th H T U	e Th H T U
6 0	2 6 0	5 4 8 0	3 0 1 0	9 5 0 0
_____	_____	_____	_____	_____

Task 3
Make each of these numbers 100 times bigger.

a 4 _____   b 69 _____

c 29 _____   d 36 _____

Make each of these numbers 100 times smaller.

e 4000 _____   f 3500 _____

g 7100 _____   h 2400 _____

Task 4
What numbers are represented here?

a XV _____

b XXIV _____

c LXI _____

d XC _____

Write these numbers in Roman numerals.

e 16 _____

f 35 _____

g 52 _____

h 26 _____

FACT FILE

Animal: Snail

Habitat: Different types of snails live on land, in fresh water and in salt water

Weight: Average weight of a garden snail is 12g

Lifespan: 2 to 3 years in the wild

Diet: Decaying plants, fruit, vegetables and algae

Exploring Further ...

Which snail did each number on the left go through to become the number on the right?

a 63   ×10   630

b 580   ÷10   58

c 6100   ×100   61

d 4350   435

e 39   ÷100   3900

WILD FACT

A snail's body is long, damp and slimy and moves on a single foot. The foot has a special gland which produces slime so that the snail can easily glide along. This leaves behind the familiar tell-tale, slimy tracks.

Now trail to pages 44–45 to record what you have learned in your explorer's logbook.

Rounding and negative numbers

Discover how good you are at rounding.

The rounding rules:

- Find the rounding digit.
- If rounding to the nearest ten, your rounding digit is in the tens column.
- If rounding to the nearest hundred, your rounding digit is in the hundreds column, and so on.
- Look at the digit immediately to the right of the rounding digit.
- If it is 1, 2, 3 or 4, the rounding digit stays the same.
- If it is 5, 6, 7, 8 or 9, the rounding digit goes up one.

Occasionally, there will be a knock-on effect to the next column on the left.

On these pages, you can also check your understanding of negative numbers. Here is a number line showing negative numbers.

```
-10   -8   -6   -4   -2   0    2    4    6    8    10
|‾|‾|‾|‾|‾|‾|‾|‾|‾|‾|‾|‾|‾|‾|‾|‾|‾|‾|‾|‾|‾|
```

Task 1	Round these numbers to the nearest ten.

a 23 _____   b 78 _____   c 35 _____

d 712 _____   e 257 _____   f 495 _____

6

Task 2 Round these numbers to the nearest hundred.

a 529 _____ b 761 _____ c 350 _____

d 2831 _____ e 7469 _____ f 8963 _____

WILD FACT

Ladybirds have two sets of wings. The coloured areas we can easily see are actually wing covers called elytra which protect the flying wings underneath.

Task 3 Round these numbers to the nearest thousand.

a 4449 _____ b 3601 _____ c 7501 _____

Task 4 Complete the following sequences.

a –4 –3 –2 ____ ____ ____ 2 ____

b ____ ____ ____ –2 0 2 ____ ____

c –12 –8 ____ ____ 4 8 ____ ____

d ____ ____ ____ –1 4 9 ____ ____

e –8 ____ ____ 1 4 7 ____ ____

WILD FACT

There are 88 species of ladybird in Northern and Central Europe alone, in various shades of yellow, red and orange with different spot patterns.

Exploring Further ...

Round the ladybirds.

	Round to the nearest 10	Round to the nearest 100	Round to the nearest 1000
3117			
5351			
2459			
4965			
4293			
3969			

Now fly to pages 44–45 to record what you have learned in your explorer's logbook.

7

Addition

Once you know your **number bonds**, you need strategies for mental **addition** to help you to deal with bigger numbers, especially when you have to bridge sets of ten.

For example: 46 + 27

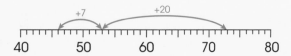

Start at 46 and add 7.

46 is 4 away from 50, so break 7 down into the number bond 4 and 3. Add 4 to get to 50 and then 3 takes you to 53.

Now add 20 to get 73.

Rounding 9s into 10s also helps. So 34 + 19 becomes 34 + 20 − 1 = 54 − 1 = 53.

When you need to add bigger numbers, you should use the columnar method.

Th	H	T	U
3	9	4	6
+ 2	8	7	9
6	8	2	5
1	1	1	

FACT FILE

Animal:	Woodlouse
Habitat:	Under bark and leaves in moist areas of gardens and woodland
Size:	Average of 1.5 cm
Lifespan:	Up to 4 years
Diet:	Decaying leaves, plants and fruits

Task 1 Find the answers to these sums mentally.

a What is the sum of 54 and 78? _____

b Add together 361 and 638. _____

c 502 plus 293 _____

d Find the sum of 843 and 239. _____

e 158 + 771 _____

WILD FACT

A woodlouse does not wee! Instead, waste water passes through the outer shell as the gas ammonia.

Solve these problems in your head.

a Susie counted 36 woodlice in her garden and Jamilla counted 47.
How many did they count altogether? _____

b James counted the number of snails on his patio at 9.30 each evening for
5 days. Here are his results: Monday – 23, Tuesday – 38, Wednesday – 12,
Thursday – 47, Friday – 20. How many did he count altogether? _____

Task 3   Calculate the answers to these
sums using the columnar method.

a

```
   4098
   2407
 + 1592
 _____

 _____
```

b

```
     32
    416
 + 5927
 _____

 _____
```

c   1008
```
      7
    624
 + 6472
 _____

 _____
```

WILD FACT

A woodlouse is a crustacean, more closely related to crabs and lobsters than to insects.

Task 4   Solve this problem using the columnar method.

b Whilst conducting a bug survey in Greenside Forest, Mary walked 3912 m,
Andrew walked 809 m further than Mary and Peter walked 753 m further
than Andrew. How far did they walk altogether?

Exploring Further ...

Three thousand three hundred and forty five of the visitors to the
woodland trail in Greenside Forest last year were adults. Jane
subtracted this number from the total number of visitors and found
that one thousand nine hundred and twenty four visitors were
children. How many visitors were there altogether last year?

_____

**Now creep to pages 44–45 to record what you have
learned in your explorer's logbook.**

Subtraction

Knowing your **number bonds** is essential to accurate **subtraction** too. If you know that 6 and 7 make 13, then it is easy to see that 13 – 7 = 6 and 13 – 6 = 7.

In a subtraction, if all the digits in the bigger number are bigger than the corresponding digits in the smaller number, the sum is easy.

For example: 693 – 471

If they are not all bigger, then bridging or exchanging will be necessary. Get used to scanning subtractions in this way.

Task 1 — Whizz through these easy sums.

a Subtract 46 from 97 _____

b 89 minus 34 _____

c Take 275 from 899 _____

d Find the difference between 126 and 337 _____

e How much more is 763 than 520? _____

Task 2   Bridging is needed in these calculations.

a 40 – 25 ____   b 85 – 39 ____   c 37 – 18 ____   d 62 – 26 ____   e 94 – 57 ____

Task 3   Set these sums out in columns.
Look for the exchanges!

a 692 – 248   b 935 – 581   c 703 – 396

WILD FACT

If a devil's coach horse beetle is disturbed, it raises its rear end like a scorpion and opens its fearsome jaws. It then squirts a foul liquid from its abdomen and can give a painful bite.

Task 4   Now try these trickier subtractions using the columnar method.

a 7986 – 4397   b 5214 – 2398

c 6802 – 1773   d 7000 – 4857

WILD FACT

The devil's coach horse beetle turns its food into a ball, then chews and passes it through its digestive system a few times until it becomes liquid.

Exploring Further ...

Beetle 1 scuttles from A to B to C.
His total journey is 7652 m. How far
is it from A to B?   _____

Beetle 2 scuttles from A to D to C.
Her total journey is 8012 m. How far
is it from D to C?   _____

Beetle 3 scuttles from A to B to D to C.
His total journey is 9000 m. How far
is it from B to D?   _____

A   B

2497 m

D

5746 m

C

**Now scuttle to pages 44–45 to record what you have
learned in your explorer's logbook.**

11

Factors and multiples

Factors and multiples are very important to your maths work.

Multiples are sets of numbers that can be divided by a number. They are equal to or more than the original number.

Factors divide into a number and are equal to or less than the original number.

12, 24, 36, 48

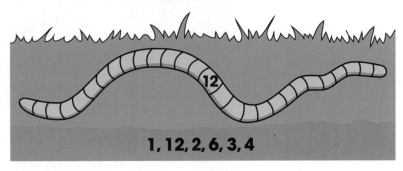

1, 12, 2, 6, 3, 4

1, 12, 2, 6, 3, 4 are factors of 12 and 12, 24, 36, 48 are multiples of 12.

FACT FILE

Animal: Earthworm

Habitat: Under or on the surface of moist soil

Size: Around 12 cm long

Lifespan: Certain species can live up to 8 years

Diet: Decaying roots, leaves and dead animals in the soil

Task 1

All of the following numbers are factors of 30.
Can you pair them up so each pair multiplies to get 30?

| 5 | 15 | 30 | 3 | 2 | 6 | 10 | 1 |

Task 2 Track down the missing factors.

a $20 = 4 \times$ _____ b $32 = 8 \times$ _____ c $16 = 2 \times$ _____ d $18 = 6 \times$ _____

Task 3 Underline numbers which are multiples of:

a **6:**   46   36   12   22   18   30

b **7:**   35   42   12   18   28   84

c **9:**   81   56   27   38   72   63

d **25:** 70   50   525   775   485   365

WILD FACT

An earthworm's body is made up of segments. It can re-grow damaged parts of its body if it isn't too badly damaged.

Task 4 Track down the missing multiples.

a **1000:** 2000   3000   _____   _____   _____   _____

b **8:**   _____   _____   32   40   _____   _____

c **7:**   _____   21   28   _____   _____   _____

d **9:**   18   _____   36   45   _____   _____

WILD FACT

A football field can have more than a million worms living in its soil.

Exploring Further ...

a Write all the factors of each number on the worms' segments:

48

| 1 | | | | | | | | 48 |

45

| 1 | | | | 45 |

42

| 1 | | | | | 42 |

b Which factors do all three worms share? _____

c Which factors are common to 48 and 42? _____

Now wriggle to pages 44–45 to record what you have learned in your explorer's logbook.

Multiplication

There are different ways to **multiply** because the order in which you multiply doesn't matter.

For example: 2 × 18 × 5.

Here it is easiest to multiply 2 by 5 first and then 10 by 18.
This is easier than 2 × 18 = 36 and then 36 × 5.

To make calculations easier, break numbers down into additions and subtractions.

For example: 62 × 3 becomes (60 × 3) + (2 × 3) = 180 + 6 = 186.

Sometimes it is quickest and easiest to use the formal method.

```
    H   T   U
    3   8   2
×           6
_____
2   2   9   2
        4   1
```

FACT FILE

Animal:	Woodworm
Habitat:	Inside trees and the wood in houses
Size:	2.7 to 4.5 mm long
Lifespan:	3 to 4 years
Diet:	Eats the wood it lives in and tunnels out

Task 1 To spot the easiest methods, you must know your table facts! Check how quickly you can recall them:

a **i)** 2 × 1 _____   **ii)** 7 × 2 _____   **iii)** 9 × 3 _____   **iv)** 11 × 3 _____

b **i)** 3 × 0 _____   **ii)** 6 × 3 _____   **iii)** 5 × 4 _____   **iv)** 10 × 4 _____

c **i)** 5 × 1 _____   **ii)** 7 × 5 _____   **iii)** 6 × 0 _____   **iv)** 6 × 8 _____

d **i)** 8 × 7 _____   **ii)** 3 × 7 _____   **iii)** 9 × 8 _____   **iv)** 6 × 9 _____

Task 2 Write down the easiest order then give the answer:

a 9 × 4 × 3 _____   **b** 2 × 12 × 5 _____

c 5 × 15 × 4 _____   **d** 8 × 6 × 5 _____

Task 3   Try these sums in two ways.

For example: $2 \times (4 + 5) = 2 \times 9 = 18$ OR
$2 \times (4 + 5) = (2 \times 4) + (2 \times 5) = 8 + 10 = 18$ _____

a   **i)** $3 \times (6 + 2) =$ _____

    ii) $5 \times (4 + 1) =$ _____

Now try these:

b   **i)** $74 \times 3 = (70 \times 3) + (4 \times 3) =$ _____ $+$ _____ $=$ _____

    ii) $49 \times 6 = ($ ___ $\times$ ___ $) + ($ ___ $\times$ ___ $) =$ _____ $+$ _____ $=$ _____

c   In these calculations, add or subtract before you multiply:

    For example: $(14 \times 5) + (14 \times 2) = 14 \times 7 = 98$
                $(24 \times 6) - (21 \times 6) = \ 3 \times 6 = 18$

    i) $(21 \times 6) + (21 \times 4) =$ _____

   ii) $(27 \times 4) - (18 \times 4) =$ _____

WILD FACT

A woodworm is the larva of the woodworm beetle (just like a caterpillar is the larva of a butterfly). It isn't a worm at all!

Task 4   Use the formal method to multiply these numbers.

a 57×9 **b** 68×6

Exploring Further ...

Stop the woodworm from munching through the wood. Find the two wrong answers and write the correct answers on the line.

$8 \times 7 = 56$	$9 \times 6 = 54$	$2 \times 8 \times 6 = 96$	$70 \times 7 = 490$
$8 \times (3 + 2) = 26$	$85 \times 3 = 255$	$6 \times (3 + 4) = 42$	$(12 \times 3) + (12 \times 2) = 72$

_____

Now munch to pages **44–45** to record what you have learned in your explorer's logbook.

Division

Division is the inverse of multiplication.

48 ÷ 6 means 'How many 6s make 48?' or 'How many sets of 6 are in 48?'

To divide accurately, you need to know your times tables very well!

For example:

270 ÷ 9

270 is ten times bigger than 27 so the answer will be ten times bigger: 27 ÷ 9 = 3 so 270 ÷ 9 = 30

800 ÷ 4

800 is a hundred times bigger than 8 so the answer will be a hundred times bigger: 8 ÷ 4 = 2 so 800 ÷ 4 = 200

On these pages, discover how well you can perform the formal method of division.

WILD FACT

Most insects do not care for their young, but the female earwig is a good mum. She feeds the young insects when they hatch until they can look after themselves.

FACT FILE

Animal: Earwig
Habitat: Under leaves, trees or in damp and dark areas of houses
Size: 10 to 14 mm long
Lifespan: Up to 3 years
Diet: Mostly plants but also greenflies, insect eggs and spiders

---

Task 1 — How well do you know your division facts?

a i) 55 ÷ 5 _____ **ii)** 8 ÷ 8 _____ **iii)** 4 ÷ 1 _____ **iv)** 15 ÷ 3 _____

b i) 48 ÷ 4 _____ **ii)** 30 ÷ 3 _____ **iii)** 64 ÷ 8 _____ **iv)** 18 ÷ 2 _____

c i) 36 ÷ 6 _____ **ii)** 36 ÷ 9 _____ **iii)** 56 ÷ 7 _____ **iv)** 44 ÷ 11 _____

d i) 72 ÷ 12 _____ **ii)** 28 ÷ 7 _____ **iii)** 108 ÷ 9 _____ **iv)** 132 ÷ 11 _____

Task 2 — Investigate dividing a multiple of 10 and 100.

a 900 ÷ 3 _____ **b** 400 ÷ 2 _____

c 450 ÷ 9 _____ **d** 720 ÷ 8 _____

WILD FACT

Female earwigs' pincers are straight and males' are curved. Earwigs have wings shaped like ears, and their original name may have been 'earwing' which then became 'earwig'. Nothing to do with human ears at all!

16

Task 3

Use the formal written method for these divisions.

a 91 ÷ 7   **b** 84 ÷ 6   **c** 936 ÷ 8   **d** 675 ÷ 5

Task 4

Now try the formal written method for these divisions.

a 637 ÷ 7   **b** 544 ÷ 8   **c** 927 ÷ 9   **d** 642 ÷ 6

Exploring Further ...

Identify the minibeasts under the leaves! If the number on the leaf will divide by 6, it is a woodlouse; if it divides by 7, it is an earwig, and if it divides by 9, it is a centipede.

Which type of minibeast is under each leaf?

 399   510   952   868

_____ _____ _____ _____

Now crawl to pages 44–45 to record what you have learned in your explorer's logbook.

Fractions

Fractions are a good opportunity to test and use your knowledge of factors and multiples. You can see from the fractions wall below that $\frac{3}{5}$ is the same as $\frac{6}{10}$.

$\frac{3}{5}$ and $\frac{6}{10}$ are **equivalent fractions**. You will notice that:

- 6 is a multiple of 3 and 10 is a multiple of 5
- 3 is a factor of 6 and 5 is a factor of 10
- 6 and 10 have a common factor of 2

Discover how well you can add and subtract fractions.

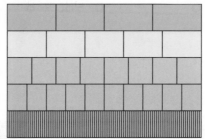

Quarters
Fifths
Eighths
Tenths
Hundredths

Task 1 Use the fractions wall to help you to find equivalent fractions.

a i) $\frac{1}{5} = \frac{}{10}$ ii) $\frac{4}{5} = \frac{}{10}$

iii) Look at each answer. What has the numerator been multiplied by to make the new fraction? _____

b i) $\frac{1}{4} = \frac{}{8}$ ii) $\frac{3}{4} = \frac{}{8}$

iii) Look at each answer. What has the numerator been multiplied by to make the new fraction? _____

c i) $\frac{1}{10} = \frac{}{100}$ ii) $\frac{7}{10} = \frac{}{100}$

iii) Look at each answer. What has the numerator been multiplied by to make the new fraction? _____

Task 2 Use the fractions wall to help you to find equivalent fractions.

a i) $\dfrac{4}{10} = \dfrac{}{5}$

ii) $\dfrac{6}{10} = \dfrac{}{5}$

iii) Look at each answer. What has the numerator been

divided by to make the new fraction? _____

b i) $\dfrac{4}{8} = \dfrac{}{4}$

ii) $\dfrac{6}{8} = \dfrac{}{4}$

iii) Look at each answer. What has the numerator been

divided by to make the new fraction? _____

c i) $\dfrac{30}{100} = \dfrac{}{10}$

ii) $\dfrac{50}{100} = \dfrac{}{10}$

iii) Look at each answer. What has the numerator been

divided by to make the new fraction? _____

Task 3 Add or subtract these fractions. Simplify your answers.

a $\dfrac{4}{9} + \dfrac{2}{9} =$

b $\dfrac{7}{8} - \dfrac{3}{8} =$

c $\dfrac{5}{12} + \dfrac{4}{12} =$

d $\dfrac{9}{10} - \dfrac{3}{10} =$

WILD FACT

A harvestman looks like a spider but isn't. Its more common name is 'daddy longlegs'. A spider has two clear body parts, but a harvestman has just one. And it only has two eyes compared to a spider's eight.

Exploring Further ...

Match a fraction at the end of harvestman A's legs with an equivalent fraction at the end of harvestman B's legs.

A

$\dfrac{3}{4}$ $\dfrac{1}{6}$ $\dfrac{5}{8}$ $\dfrac{2}{5}$ $\dfrac{1}{2}$ $\dfrac{3}{7}$ $\dfrac{2}{3}$ $\dfrac{7}{10}$

B

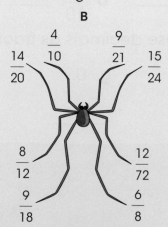

$\dfrac{4}{10}$ $\dfrac{9}{21}$ $\dfrac{14}{20}$ $\dfrac{15}{24}$ $\dfrac{8}{12}$ $\dfrac{12}{72}$ $\dfrac{9}{18}$ $\dfrac{6}{8}$

Now spin to pages 44–45 to record what you have learned in your explorer's logbook.

Decimals

Thousands, Hundreds, Tens and Units all represent whole numbers. In the **decimal system**, we also need to divide our whole units into fractions which are based on tens. In the decimal columns, 't' represents tenths and 'h' represents hundredths. The decimal point(.) separates the fractions from the whole units:

Th   H   T   U   .   t   h

For example: $0.3 = \frac{3}{10}$ = three tenths, $0.30 = \frac{30}{100}$ = thirty hundredths and $0.03 = \frac{3}{100}$ = three hundredths

You must learn these facts:

- ten tenths = 1 whole one
- one hundred hundredths = 1 whole one
- ten hundredths = 1 tenth
- $0.5 = \frac{5}{10} = \frac{1}{2}$
- $0.25 = \frac{25}{100} = \frac{1}{4}$
- $0.75 = \frac{75}{100} = \frac{3}{4}$

FACT FILE

Animal:	Pond skater
Habitat:	Still waters such as ponds, streams and marshes
Size:	8 to 20 mm long
Lifespan:	1 to 6 months
Diet:	Small insects on the water's surface

Task 1   Write these fractions as decimals.

a $\frac{3}{10}$ _____   b $\frac{7}{10}$ _____   c $\frac{45}{100}$ _____   d $\frac{36}{100}$ _____   e $\frac{1}{2}$ _____

Write these decimals as fractions.

f   0.9   g   0.1   h   0.6   i   0.87   j   0.25

_____   _____   _____   _____   _____

Task 2

Make these numbers 10x bigger. Remember each digit moves one place to the left.

a 3.4 _____ b 5.9 _____ c 7.31 _____ d 4.02 _____

Make these numbers 10x smaller. Each digit moves one place to the right.

e 61 _____ f 82 _____ g 25.7 _____ h 1.3 _____

Make these numbers 100x bigger.

i 2.64 _____ j 4.92 _____ k 8.3 _____ l 0.2 _____

Make these numbers 100x smaller.

m 349 _____ n 681 _____ o 56 _____ p 43 _____

Task 3

What is the value of the underlined digit?

a 5.6_9 _____ b 8.4_ _____ c 6.0_1 _____ d 45.1_3 _____

Task 4

Round these numbers to the nearest whole number.

a 4.2 _____ b 5.9 _____

c 1.5 _____ d 46.3 _____

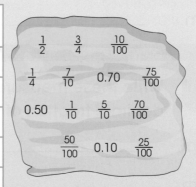

WILD FACT

The pond skater can jump 50 cm into the air and it can reach speeds of 35–125 cm per second! Its mouth is like a dagger. It pierces its prey and sucks out the body fluids, leaving the skin behind.

Exploring Further ...

Which pond skater gets the furthest? Fill the gaps in the table with as many equivalent fractions and decimals as you can from the pond. An example has been done for you.

		0.8	$\frac{8}{10}$	$\frac{8}{100}$	$\frac{4}{5}$	0.80
a	0.5					
b	0.1					
c	0.25					
d	0.75					
e	0.7					

$\frac{1}{2}$ $\frac{3}{4}$ $\frac{10}{100}$

$\frac{1}{4}$ $\frac{7}{10}$ 0.70 $\frac{75}{100}$

0.50 $\frac{1}{10}$ $\frac{5}{10}$ $\frac{70}{100}$

$\frac{50}{100}$ 0.10 $\frac{25}{100}$

Now skate to pages 44–45 to record what you have learned in your explorer's logbook.

Length

WILD FACT

Grasshoppers first lived on the Earth about 220 million years ago.

You need to know how to convert one unit of **length** into another:

10 mm = 1 cm   100 cm = 1 m

Changing from a bigger unit (like a metre) into a smaller one (like centimetres) requires multiplication because there will be more of the smaller units.

$4.34 \text{ m} = 4 \text{ m } \frac{34}{100} \text{ m} = 4 \text{ m} + 34 \text{ cm} = 434 \text{ cm}$

$4.34 \times 100 = 434 \text{ cm}$

Converting from a smaller unit to a bigger one requires division.

$86 \text{ mm} = 8 \text{ cm} + 6 \text{ mm} = 8 \frac{6}{10} \text{ cm} = 8.6 \text{ cm}$

$86 \text{ mm} = 86 \div 10 = 8.6 \text{ cm}$

FACT FILE

Animal: Grasshopper
Habitat: Dry, open and grassy places such as meadows and fields
Size: 1 to 7 cm long
Lifespan: 3 to 12 months
Diet: Mostly grasses such as corn, wheat and barley

Task 1   Write these measures as a fraction of a centimetre and as a decimal fraction of a centimetre e.g. 3 mm = $\frac{3}{10}$ cm = 0.3 cm

a 1 mm   _____   b 7 mm   _____

c 9 mm   _____   d 21 mm   _____

Task 2   Write these measures as a fraction of a metre and as a decimal fraction of a metre e.g. 17 cm = $\frac{17}{100}$ m = 0.17 m

a 43 cm   _____   b 57 cm   _____

c 21 cm   _____   d 189 cm   _____

Task 3

Perimeter is the distance all the way round the outside.

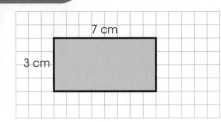

The perimeter of this rectangle is
7 cm + 3 cm + 7 cm + 3 cm = 20 cm
OR 2 x (7 cm + 3 cm) = 2 x 10 = 20 cm
The perimeter of a rectangle is often written
as 2(length + width)

Find the perimeter of these shapes.

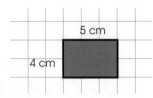

a

_____

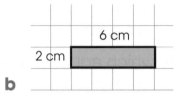

b

_____

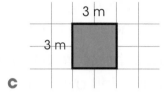

c

_____

Task 4

Area is a measure which finds how much space is inside a shape. By counting the squares, find the area of these shapes:

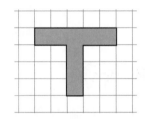

a

_____

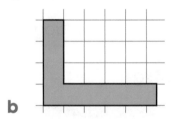

b

_____

WILD FACT

Grasshoppers make a sound called 'stridulation'. They do this by rubbing a ridged part of their back legs against a ridged part of their wings.

Exploring Further ...

On a bug hunt, Nicole and Mo collected and measured some creatures. Nicole measured hers in millimetres and Mo measured his in centimetres. Help them to compare their results. Find the difference in length of each creature in mm and in cm.

	Nicole's creatures	Mo's creatures	Difference in mm	Difference in cm
Centipede	5 mm	1 cm		
Devil's coach horse beetle	25 mm	2.7 cm		
Earthworm	85 mm	7 cm		
Millipede	9 mm	1.4 cm		
Grasshopper	57 mm	3 cm		

Now hop to pages 44–45 to record what you have learned in your explorer's logbook.

Weight

Can you remember the facts about **weight**?

1000 mg = 1 gram, 1000 g = 1 kg, 1000 kg = 1t

When converting between different measures of weight, you only need to think about sets of a thousand.

In 5912 g there are 5 thousands, which equals 5 kg and 912 grams left over. So 5912 g = 5 kg 912 g.

In 6t 12 kg, 6t = 6000 kg. Adding in the 12 kg gives 6012 kg.

Take care with your place value in these conversions.

Task 1

Match each animal to the most appropriate measure of weight.

elephant   dog   aphid

1 mg   13 kg   3 tonnes

Task 2

Change these measures into kilograms and grams
e.g. 3910 g = 3 kg 910 g

a 2731 g _____   **b** 5802 g _____

c 6091 g _____   **d** 4400 g _____

Change these measures into tonnes and kilograms e.g. 2841 kg = 2t 841 kg

e 9263 kg _____   **f** 4905 kg _____

g 8012 kg _____   **h** 3200 kg _____

Task 3

Change these measures into grams e.g. 3 kg 40 g = 3040 grams

a 5 kg 500 g _____   **b** 8 kg 86 g _____

c 4 kg 9 g _____   **d** 2 kg 349 g _____

Task 4

Change these measures into milligrams e.g. 9 g 9 mg = 9009 mg

a 8 g 274 mg _____   **b** 3 g 700 mg _____

c 5 g 24 mg _____   **d** 7 g 2 mg _____

Task 5

Put these weights in order starting with the heaviest.

a 721 g   721 kg   7210 g   7 kg 2 g   7201 kg   7 t 70 kg

_____

b 4035 mg   4 g   4003 g   4 g 5 mg   3 kg 54 g   3045 g

_____

Exploring Further ...

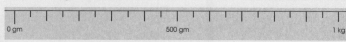

0 gm   500 gm   1 kg

a A biologist has calculated that 175 thousand aphids would weigh just 350 grams. Show this weight on the scale above.

↓

0 kg   5 kg   10 kg   15 kg

b He also calculated that 175 thousand aphids would produce several kilograms of sugary sap in one month. Look at the weight he estimated on the scale above and round it to the nearest kilogram.

_____

Now fly to pages 44–45 to record what you have learned in your explorer's logbook.

Capacity

FACT FILE

Animal: Stick insect
Habitat: Forests and grasslands
Size: Up to 33 cm long
Lifespan: Up to 3 years in the wild
Diet: Leaves, plants and berries

The standard unit of **capacity** is the litre. There are 1000 ml in one litre. There is also a measure of capacity called the centilitre. You will not come across it very often but it's good to know that
100 centilitres = 1 litre
and 10 ml = 1 centilitre.

Task 1

Look at the following containers. What is **i)** the exact reading and **ii)** the reading to the nearest litre.

a

b
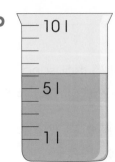

i) _____

ii) _____

i) _____

ii) _____

Task 2

Look at these containers. How many centilitres need to be added to make 1 litre?

a
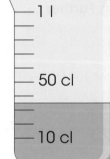

b
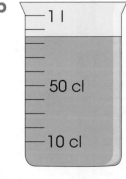

_____

_____

26

Task 3

How much needs to be taken out of each container to make 500 ml?

a

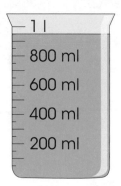

1 l
800 ml
600 ml
400 ml
200 ml

_____

b

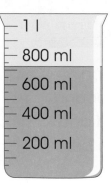

1 l
800 ml
600 ml
400 ml
200 ml

_____

Task 4

Put in order from smallest to biggest.

a 7500 cl   75 ml   75 cl   7505 ml   755 ml   7.5 l

_____

b 47 ml   4 l   401 cl   4001 ml   4.1 l   410 ml

_____

WILD FACT

A stick insect looks exactly like a twig with legs. It usually adopts the colour of its surroundings, making perfect camouflage in leaves. Even stick insect eggs look like seeds.

WILD FACT

If a predator grabs a stick insect's leg, it can detach the leg from its body and then grow another one. It can also produce a foul smell to discourage predators from eating it.

Exploring Further ...

Match the pairs which make 2 litres together.

50 cl

1.2 l

80 cl

1500 ml

100 cl

60 cl

200 ml

1400 ml

1800 ml

1 l

Now crawl to pages 44–45 to record what you have learned in your explorer's logbook.

Money

In the UK, the **money** system is based on decimals. There are 100 pennies in a pound which means that 1p is $\frac{1}{100}$ of a pound and 10p is $\frac{1}{10}$ of a pound. Money can also be written as decimals of a pound:

1p = £0.01, 10p = £0.10, 35p = £0.35, £7 and 32p = £7.32.

The decimal point is usually known as the pennies point. There are two important rules when writing amounts of money in pounds.

1. There should always be two digits after the pennies point

2. Never write the p sign when you have the £ sign and the pennies point.

Task 1
Write the following amounts as decimals of a pound.

a 89p _____   b 46p _____

c 30p _____   d 5p _____

e £6 and 78 pence _____   f £1 and 2 pence _____

Task 2
Calculate how many pence there are in the following amounts.

a £5.90 _____   b £8.09 _____

c £4.36 _____   d £10.02 _____

Task 3

Match the pairs which make £1 together. Colour the matching amounts using the same colour.

a (32p) (74p) (42p) (23p) (58p) (87p) (26p) (77p) (36p) (64p) (13p) (68p)

Match the pairs which make £5 together.

b (£3.15) (£3.40) (£2.15) (£0.60) (£4.49) (£1.85) (£1.60) (£0.51) (£2.85) (£4.40)

Task 4

Write down the change you would get from £2 using the amounts in the box.

| £1.90 | £1.28 | £1.01 | 90p | 83p | £1.18 | 91p | £2.28 | 73p |

I spend a £1.27 _____   b £0.82 _____

c £1.09 _____   d £0.10 _____

WILD FACT

There are about 3500 different species of cockroach. They are very adaptable so are found in every corner of the world.

Exploring Further ...

Jodie is planning a country holiday with her husband and three children for 5 nights. Which is the cheapest option?

Greenside Forest Pine Lodge Holidays	Beechdale Woodland Holidays	Medlock Country Retreats
Adults £65 per night Children £40 per night	1 adult & 1 child £98 per night Extra child £50 per night	5 night special 2 adults & 2 children £1000 Extra child £47 per night

Now scuttle to pages 44–45 to record what you have learned in your explorer's logbook.

Time

Time isn't an easy measure because there are many different facts to remember, and we write time in different ways too.

Analogue time is when you read the time from a clock with moving hands.

Digital time is when you read the time from a clock which only shows numbers.

Check your facts:

60 seconds = 1 minute

60 minutes = 1 hour

24 hours = 1 day

7 days = 1 week

12 months = 1 year

Task 1

Match the analogue time on the left with the correct digital time on the right.

a 5 past 6 in the morning   20:45

b quarter to 9 in the evening   06:05

c quarter past 3 in the afternoon   07:54

d 25 minutes to 2 in the afternoon   15:15

e 6 minutes to 8 in the morning   13:35

WILD FACT

When they are in danger, millipedes curl into tiny balls and some species give off a smelly, poisonous liquid from glands on their sides. Some tropical millipedes can produce light, like fireflies.

FACT FILE

Animal: Millipede

Habitat: Beneath wood, rocks, leaves or in soil

Size: 2 to 6 cm long

Lifespan: Some species can live up to 7 years

Diet: Decaying wood and vegetation

Task 2 Write these 12 hour clock times as 24 hour clock times.

a 11.43 pm _____   **b** 11.21 am _____   **c** 8.13 am _____

d 6.57 pm _____   **e** 1.25 pm _____

WILD FACT

Task 3 Mrs Higham says, 'Our train arrives home at 19:35.'

Which of her children are correct?

Peter says, 'That's 25 to 7 in the evening.'

Paula says, 'No, that's 7.35 in the evening.'

Philip says, 'No, it's 25 to 8 in the evening.'

Patricia says, 'No, it's 35 minutes past seven in the evening.'

_____

The name millipede means 'a thousand feet', but no millipede has that many feet. Millipedes have two pairs of legs on each segment of their body.

Task 4 Solve these calculations.

a How many minutes are there in 7 hours?   _____

b How many seconds are there in 30 minutes?   _____

c How many months are there in 9 years?   _____

d How many days are there in 8 weeks?   _____

Exploring Further ...

Write the numbers in these sentences in a more sensible way:

a The millipede's eggs hatched 35 days after being laid. The millipede's eggs hatched _____ weeks after being laid.

b A millipede can live for 84 months. A millipede can live for _____ years.

c It took me 240 seconds to find some millipedes in my garden. It took me _____ minutes to find some millipedes in my garden.

Now creep to pages 44–45 to record what you have learned in your explorer's logbook.

Angles

The v-shaped space created when two straight lines meet or cross is called an **angle**.
Angles are measured in degrees °.

- A right angle or square corner measures 90°.

- A straight line is equal to 2 right angles or 180°.

- An angle which is smaller than a right angle (less than 90°) is called acute.

- An angle which is bigger than a right angle but less than 2 right angles (more than 90° but less than 180°) is called obtuse.

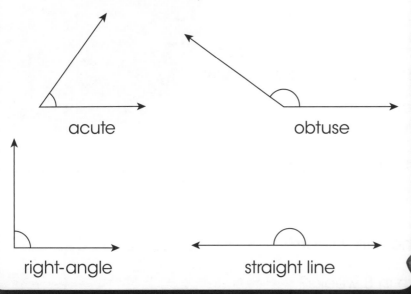

acute   obtuse

right-angle   straight line

Task 1   State whether each marked angle is acute, obtuse or a right angle.

a   b   c   d

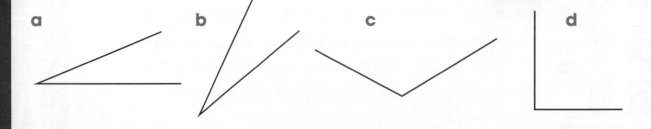

_____   _____   _____   _____

Task 2   State whether each of these angles is acute, obtuse or a right angle.

a 36° _____

b 91° _____

c 175° _____

d 90° _____

e 12° _____

f 87° _____

Task 3   Put these angles in order of size, starting with the smallest

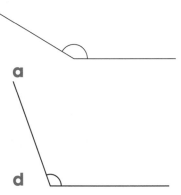
a

b

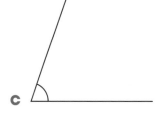
c

d

e

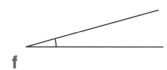
f

_____

Exploring Further ...

State whether the angles in each of the following shapes are equal or unequal.

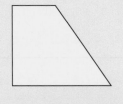
a

_____

b

_____

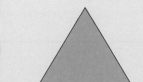
c

_____

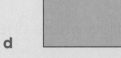
d

_____

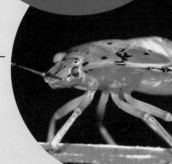

Now flit to pages 44–45 to record what you have learned in your explorer's logbook.

2D shapes

Bugs and insects are usually described by how many legs they have, whether their bodies are segmented or not, whether they have wings and so on. These are called characteristics. **2D shapes** have characteristics too, which we call properties. The properties of 2D shapes are:

- The number of sides.

- The number of angles.

- Whether the sides are straight or curved.

- The lengths of the sides and whether or not they are equal. The word 'regular' is used for a 2D shape with all sides equal and 'irregular' means the sides are unequal.

- Whether any sides are parallel.

Look at these triangles and quadrilaterals, and learn their names and properties:

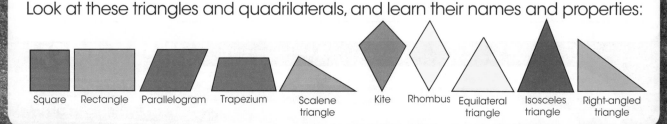

Square Rectangle Parallelogram Trapezium Scalene triangle Kite Rhombus Equilateral triangle Isosceles triangle Right-angled triangle

---

Task 1 **Answer these questions about triangles.**

a Is a scalene triangle a regular or an irregular shape? _____

b Which triangle has three equal sides and three equal angles? _____

c How many equal sides does an isosceles triangle have? _____

d What is a triangle called where one of the angles is 90°? _____

Task 2

Look at the quadrilaterals in the introduction and write each name in the correct place in the grid. Put a cross in any empty boxes.

	Two pairs of parallel sides	One pair of parallel sides	No parallel sides
4 right angles			
2 acute and 2 obtuse angles			

Exploring Further ...

Put the letter of each shape into the correct place in the grid below. Put a cross in any empty boxes.

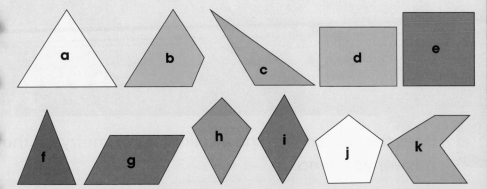

	3 sides	4 sides	More than 4 sides
2 pairs of equal sides			
2 equal sides only			
All sides equal	a		
No equal sides			

Now crawl to pages 44–45 to record what you have learned in your explorer's logbook.

35

Symmetry

Butterflies are **symmetrical**, so one half is an exact reflection of the other. Shapes are symmetrical when you can fold them in half and both halves match exactly. Imagine that one half is covered in wet paint. When you fold it over, if it is symmetrical, it makes an exact mirror image. The line of the fold is called the line of symmetry and is often shown as a dotted line.

WILD FACT

The female butterfly lays up to 500 eggs at once on the underside of stinging nettle leaves. The green and white eggs hatch into caterpillars after 10 days. The caterpillars spin a silky tent around themselves. When fully grown, they make a pupa and, after about two weeks, emerge as a butterfly.

Task 1 Does the dotted line show a line of symmetry on these shapes? Answer yes or no.

a 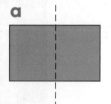 b 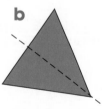 c 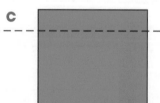 d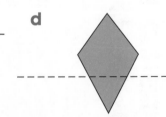

| Task 2 | Which of the following shapes are symmetrical? Put a tick in the box. |

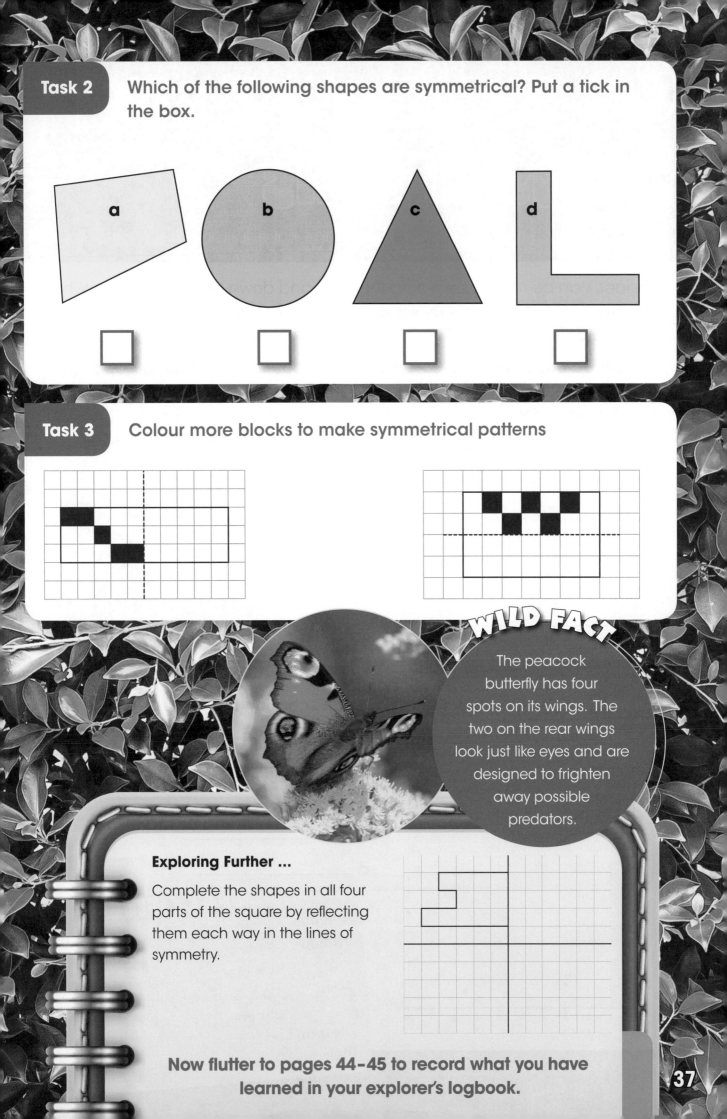

a   □
b   □
c   □
d   □

| Task 3 | Colour more blocks to make symmetrical patterns |

WILD FACT

The peacock butterfly has four spots on its wings. The two on the rear wings look just like eyes and are designed to frighten away possible predators.

Exploring Further ...

Complete the shapes in all four parts of the square by reflecting them each way in the lines of symmetry.

Now flutter to pages 44–45 to record what you have learned in your explorer's logbook.

Co-ordinates and translations

Shapes can be moved by sliding them up and down or right and left. When a shape is moved in this way without turning or changing it, it is called a **translation**.

We use **co-ordinates** to describe a shape's position on squared paper: (5, 4) The first number describes how far along and the second number describes how far up or down.

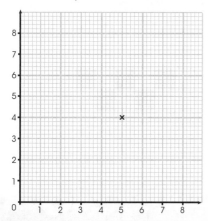

Task 1   Give the co-ordinates of each scorpion fly.

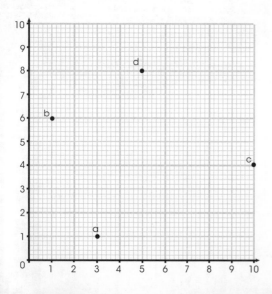

a _____

b _____

c _____

d _____

Task 2

Describe the movement of the scorpion fly(s). State how many squares left or right it needs to move and then how many squares up or down to reach its prey(p).

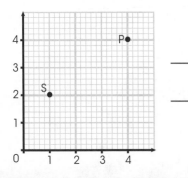

_____

_____

Task 3

Put a cross on each of the following points:

a (3, 6)   **b** (7, 1)   **c** (5, 2)

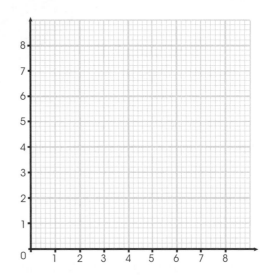

WILD FACT

You will be pleased to know that the scorpion fly does not use its tail to sting. In fact it does not kill anything, preferring to eat dead insects, especially those it can find in spiders' webs.

Exploring Further ...

Plot the following points: A (2, 5), B (8, 5), C (2, 2). With a ruler, join A to B and A to C. Point D will complete a rectangle. Give the co-ordinates of point D and complete the rectangle.

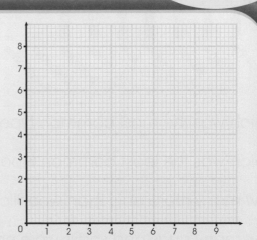

Now fly to pages 44–45 to record what you have learned in your explorer's logbook.

Statistics

Statistics is a part of mathematics for handling information or **data**. We can collect information on almost anything – how many children in your class like certain TV programmes, how fast your friends can run 100 m, the numbers of birds visiting a garden, and so on. Information collected can be presented in various ways to make it easier to understand and to make conclusions about it.

WILD FACT

Horseflies are among the largest flies in the world.

Task 1

Year 3 counted how many different kinds of bugs and insects they could find in the school garden in 15 minutes. They presented their results in a bar chart.

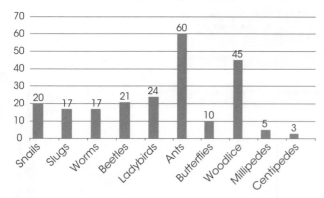

Year 3's bug count

FACT FILE

Animal:	Horsefly
Habitat:	Fields and hedgerows near water
Size:	8 to 23 mm
Lifespan:	A few days as an adult fly
Diet:	Females: mammals' blood; males: nectar

a Which was the most common type of bug seen? _____

b Which was the least common type of bug seen? _____

c How many more ants than woodlice were counted? _____

d How many slugs and snails were counted altogether? _____

Task 2

Year 4 conducted a survey of aphids on the class geranium plant. Every Monday they counted how many aphids they could see and then made monthly totals. They made a line graph of their results.

Number of aphids on Year 4's geranium plant

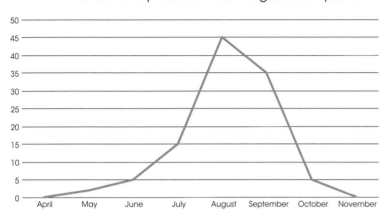

a In which month were most aphids seen? _____

b How many more aphids were counted in August than in September? _____

c In which month was the number of aphids the same as in June? _____

d In which month was the number of aphids twenty more than in July? _____

Exploring Further ...

Rhianna and George went pond dipping. They decided to make a bar chart from their findings. Rhianna has entered her results.

Can you help George to draw the bars for his findings?

Pond dipping survey

Caddis fly larva

Pond skater

Water boatman

Diving beetle

0   2   4   6   8   10   12

Caddis fly larva: 2,
Water boatman: 11,
Pond skater: 7,
Diving beetle: 3

Which creature did they count most of altogether?

_____

Now fly to pages 44–45 to record what you have learned in your explorer's logbook.

Quick test

Now try these questions. Give yourself 1 mark for every correct answer – but only if you answer each part of the question correctly!

1 Lucy counted 4073 earthworms in her garden during May.

   a Write this number in words. _____

   b What is the value of the digit 7? _____

2 Jo and Nam looked for centipedes. Jo's longest centipede measured 11mm. Nam's longest one was ten times longer than Jo's. What did Nam's centipede measure in cm? _____

3 There are about 90 species of ladybird. The exact number of species of ladybird has been rounded to the nearest ten. Complete this sentence: The number of species of ladybird ranges from _____ to _____.

4 Two schools collected money for charity. Key Stage 1 at Firdale Primary School collected £792 and Key Stage 2 collected £1079. Woodrow School collected £3042 altogether. How much more did Woodrow collect than Firdale? _____

5 James counted 9 spiders' egg sacs around his window frames. He estimated that there must be about 875 eggs in each pouch. He also estimated that about 630 eggs from each pouch would actually become spiders. How many eggs in total would NOT survive? _____

6 Write down the numbers on these snails:

   XII   XXIV   XXXVI   XVIII   LIV   XLVIII

   _____

7 A harvestman has eight legs. How many legs would 752 harvestmen have? _____

8 Oldacre Forest has an area of 8982 square metres. It was divided equally between six wardens. How many square metres did each warden care for? _____

9 Out of four hundred and eighty insects counted in a bug hunt, $\frac{1}{8}$ were earthworms and $\frac{4}{5}$ were woodlice. How many **a)** earthworms and **b)** woodlice were counted? _____

10 If a pond skater moved at a speed of 35 cm per second, how far would it travel in 30 seconds? Give your answer as a decimal of a metre. _____

11 A grasshopper of length 2.5 cm jumped 20 times its length in a single jump. How far in **a)** cm **b)** mm and **c)** m did it jump?

_____

12 Here are the weights of four insects: bumble bee – 390 mg, red admiral butterfly – 250 mg, peacock butterfly – 230 mg, dragonfly – 900 mg. Calculate their total weight in grams and milligrams. _____

13 My pond contains 11 250 litres of water. I need to treat my fish for a fungal infection. Here is a guide to how much anti-fungal liquid to put into my pond.

- 1 litre of liquid treats 9000 litres of water
- 250 ml of liquid treats 2250 litres of water
- Bottles of anti-fungal liquid contain 250 ml.

   How many bottles do I need to buy? _____

14 Put these amounts of money in order starting with the smallest.
   £45   405p   £0.45   £4.50   £4.45   £40.00   54p

_____

15 Write these analogue times as digital times.

a _____   b _____   c _____

16 Draw one line of symmetry on each shape.

Explorer's Logbook

Tick off the topics as you complete them and then colour in the star.

How do you feel?
- Needs practice
- Nearly there
- Got it!

Factors and multiples ☐

Division ☐

Multiplication ☐

Fractions ☐

Subtraction ☐

Place value ☐

Rounding and negative numbers ☐

More place value ☐

Addition ☐

Decimals ☐

2D shapes ☐

Symmetry ☐

Co-ordinates and translations ☐

Time ☐

Money ☐

Statistics ☐

Length ☐

Weight ☐

Capacity ☐

Angles ☐

45

Answers

Pages 2–3

Task 1
a 3 units, 3   **b** 6 hundredths, 600
c 7 tens, 70   **d** 8 thousandths, 8000

Task 2
a seven thousand and nine
b two thousand nine hundred and eighty
c one thousand two hundred and six
d 3420   **e** 4004   **f** 8030

Task 3
a 7899 < 7989   **b** 3072 > 3027
c 1489 < 1894
d 2121, 1221, 1201, 1112, 1102, 1012
e 5554, 5545, 5504, 5454, 5445, 5050

Task 4
a 7709   **b** 6061   **c** 1990
d 3862   **e** 7091   **f** 845

Exploring Further...
Left legs: 6044, 7044, 7344, 7444, 7454
Right legs: 6201, 6191, 6091, 5791, 4791

Pages 4–5

Task 1
a 50   **b** 920   **c** 6810   **d** 4050   **e** 7900

Task 2
a 6   **b** 26   **c** 548   **d** 301   **e** 950

Task 3
a 400   **b** 6900   **c** 2900   **d** 3600
e 40   **f** 35   **g** 71   **h** 24

Task 4
a 15   **b** 24   **c** 61   **d** 90
e XVI   **f** XXXV   **g** LII   **h** XXVI

Exploring Further...
a x10   **b** ÷10   **c** ÷100   **d** ÷10   **e** x100

Pages 6–7

Task 1
a 20   **b** 80   **c** 40   **d** 710   **e** 260   **f** 500

Task 2
a 500   **b** 800   **c** 400   **d** 2800   **e** 7500   **f** 9000

Task 3
a 4000   **b** 4000   **c** 8000

Task 4
a −4, −3, −2, −1, 0, 1, 2, 3
b −8, −6, −4, −2, 0, 2, 4, 6
c −12, −8, −4, 0, 4, 8, 12, 16
d −16, −11, −6, −1, 4, 9, 14, 19
e −8, −5, −2, 1, 4, 7, 10, 13

Exploring Further...

	Round to the nearest ten	Round to the nearest hundred	Round to the nearest thousand
3117	3120	3100	3000
5351	5350	5400	5000
2459	2460	2500	2000
4965	4970	5000	5000
4293	4290	4300	4000
3969	3970	4000	4000

Pages 8–9

Task 1
a 132   **b** 999   **c** 795   **d** 1082   **e** 929

Task 2
a 83   **b** 140

Task 3
a 8097   **b** 6375   **c** 8111

Task 4
Andrew: 4721, Peter: 5474, altogether: 14 107

Exploring Further...
3345 + 1924 = 5269

Pages 10–11

Task 1
a 51   **b** 55   **c** 624   **d** 211   **e** 243

Task 2
a 15   **b** 46   **c** 19   **d** 36   **e** 37

Task 3
a 444   **b** 354   **c** 307

Task 4
a 3589   **b** 2816   **c** 5029   **d** 2143

Exploring Further...
AB = 1906 m   DC = 5515 m
AB + DC = 7421 m   BD = 9000 − 7421 = 1579 m

Pages 12–13

Task 1
1 and 30, 2 and 15, 3 and 10, 5 and 6

Task 2
a 5   **b** 4   **c** 8   **d** 3

Task 3
a 36, 12, 18, 30   **b** 35, 42, 28, 84
c 81, 27, 72, 63   **d** 50, 525, 775

Task 4
a 2000   3000   4000   5000   6000   7000
b 16   24   32   40   48   56
c 14   21   28   35   42   49
d 18   27   36   45   54   63

Exploring Further...

a 48

```
1  2  3  4  6  8  12  16  24  48
```

45

```
1  3  5  9  15  45
```

42

```
1  2  3  6  7  14  21  42
```

b 1 and 3

c 1, 2, 3 and 6

Pages 14–15

Task 1

a i 2   ii 14   iii 27   iv 33

b i 0   ii 18   iii 20   iv 40

c i 5   ii 35   iii 0   iv 48

d i 56   ii 21   iii 72   iv 54

Task 2

a $4 \times 3 \times 9 = 108$ **b** $2 \times 5 \times 12 = 120$

c $5 \times 4 \times 15 = 300$ **d** $8 \times 5 \times 6$ OR $5 \times 6 \times 8 = 240$

Task 3

a i $3 \times (6 + 2) = 3 \times 8 = 24$ OR

     $3 \times (6 + 2) = (3 \times 6) + (3 \times 2) = 24$

   ii $5 \times (4 + 1) = 5 \times 5 = 25$ OR

     $5 \times (4 + 1) = (5 \times 4) + (5 \times 1) = 25$

b i $74 \times 3 = (70 \times 3) + (4 \times 3) = 210 + 12 = 222$

   ii $49 \times 6 = (40 \times 6) + (9 \times 6) = 240 + 54 = 294$

c i $(21 \times 6) + (21 \times 4) = 21 \times 10 = 210$

   ii $(27 \times 4) - (18 \times 4) = 9 \times 4 = 36$

Task 4

a 513   **b** 408

Exploring Further...

$(12 \times 3) + (12 \times 2) = 72$	$8 \times (3 + 2) = 26$	are incorrect
$(12 \times 3) + (12 \times 2) = 60$	$8 \times (3 + 2) = 8 \times 5 = 40$	are the correct answers

Pages 16–17

Task 1

a i 11   ii 1   iii 4   iv 5

b i 12   ii 10   iii 8   iv 9

c i 6   ii 4   iii 8   iv 4

d i 6   ii 4   iii 12   iv 12

Task 2

a 300   **b** 200   **c** 50   **d** 90

Task 3

a 13   **b** 14   **c** 117   **d** 135

Task 4

a 91   **b** 68   **c** 103   **d** 107

Exploring Further...

$399 \div 7 = 57$ Earwig $510 \div 6 = 85$ Woodlouse

$952 \div 7 = 136$ Earwig $868 \div 7 = 124$ Earwig

Pages 18–19

Task 1

a i $\frac{1}{5} = \frac{2}{10}$ ii $\frac{4}{5} = \frac{8}{10}$ iii 2

b i $\frac{1}{4} = \frac{2}{8}$ ii $\frac{3}{4} = \frac{6}{8}$ iii 2

c i $\frac{1}{10} = \frac{10}{100}$ ii $\frac{7}{10} = \frac{70}{100}$ iii 10

Task 2

a i $\frac{4}{10} = \frac{2}{5}$ ii $\frac{6}{10} = \frac{3}{5}$ iii 2

b i $\frac{4}{8} = \frac{2}{4}$ ii $\frac{6}{8} = \frac{3}{4}$ iii 2

c i $\frac{30}{100} = \frac{3}{10}$ ii $\frac{50}{100} = \frac{5}{10}$ iii 10

Task 3

a $\frac{6}{9} = \frac{2}{3}$ **b** $\frac{4}{8} = \frac{1}{2}$ **c** $\frac{9}{12} = \frac{3}{4}$ **d** $\frac{6}{10} = \frac{3}{5}$

Exploring Further...

$\frac{3}{4} = \frac{6}{8}$ $\frac{1}{6} = \frac{12}{72}$

$\frac{2}{5} = \frac{4}{10}$ $\frac{5}{8} = \frac{15}{24}$

$\frac{1}{2} = \frac{9}{18}$ $\frac{3}{7} = \frac{9}{21}$

$\frac{2}{3} = \frac{8}{12}$ $\frac{7}{10} = \frac{14}{20}$

Pages 20–21

Task 1

a 0.3   **b** 0.7   **c** 0.45   **d** 0.36   **e** 0.5

f $\frac{9}{10}$ **g** $\frac{1}{10}$ **h** $\frac{3}{5}$ **i** $\frac{87}{100}$ **j** $\frac{1}{4}$

Task 2

a 34   **b** 59   **c** 73.1   **d** 40.2   **e** 6.1

f 8.2   **g** 2.57   **h** 0.13   **i** 264   **j** 492

k 830   **l** 20   **m** 3.49   **n** 6.81   **o** 0.56

p 0.43

Task 3

a 6 tenths, $\frac{6}{10}$ **b** 4 tenths, $\frac{4}{10}$

c 1 hundredth, $\frac{1}{100}$ **d** 3 hundredths, $\frac{3}{100}$

Task 4

a 4   **b** 6   **c** 2   **d** 46

Exploring Further...

	0.8	$\frac{8}{10}$	$\frac{80}{100}$	$\frac{4}{5}$	0.80
a	0.5	$\frac{1}{2}$	0.50	$\frac{5}{10}$	$\frac{50}{100}$
b	0.1	$\frac{10}{100}$	0.10	$\frac{1}{10}$	
c	0.25	$\frac{1}{4}$	$\frac{25}{100}$		
d	0.75	$\frac{3}{4}$	$\frac{75}{100}$		
e	0.7	$\frac{7}{10}$	0.70	$\frac{70}{100}$	

Pond skater a gets the furthest.

Pages 22–23

Task 1

a $\frac{1}{10}$ cm = 0.1 cm   **b** $\frac{7}{10}$ cm = 0.7 cm

c $\frac{9}{10}$ cm = 0.9 cm   **d** $2\frac{1}{10}$ cm = 2.1 cm

Task 2

a $\frac{43}{100}$ m = 0.43 m   **b** $\frac{57}{100}$ m = 0.57 m

c $\frac{21}{100}$ m = 0.21 m   **d** $1\frac{89}{100}$ m = 1.89 m

Task 3

a $2(5 + 4)$ cm = 18 cm   **b** $2(6 + 2)$ cm = 16 cm

c 4×3 m = 12 m

Task 4

a 8 squares   **b** $8\frac{1}{2}$ squares

Exploring Further...

	Nicole's creatures	Mo's creatures	Difference in mm	Difference in cm
Centipede	5 mm	1 cm	5 mm	0.5 cm
Devil's coach horse beetle	25 mm	2.7 cm	2 mm	0.2 cm
Earthworm	85 mm	7 cm	15 mm	1.5 cm
Millipede	9 mm	1.4 cm	5 mm	0.5 cm
Grasshopper	57 mm	3 cm	27 mm	2.7 cm

Pages 24–25

Task 1
Elephant: 3 t; Dog: 13 kg; Aphid: 1 mg

Task 2
a 2 kg 731 g **b** 5 kg 802 g **c** 6 kg 91 g
d 4 kg 400 g **e** 9 t 263 kg **f** 4 t 905 kg
g 8 t 12 kg **h** 3 t 200 kg

Task 3
a 5500 g **b** 8086 g **c** 4009 g **d** 2349 g

Task 4
a 8274 mg **b** 3700 mg **c** 5024 mg **d** 7002 mg

Task 5
a 7201 kg, 7 t 70 kg, 721 kg, 7210 g, 7 kg 2 g, 721 g
b 4003 g, 3 kg 54 g, 3045 g, 4035 mg, 4 g 5 mg, 4 g

Exploring Further...
a

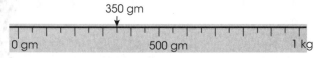

b 7 kg

Pages 26–27

Task 1
a i 1 l 750 ml **ii** 2 litres **b i** 6 l 250 ml **ii** 6 litres

Task 2
a 65 cl **b** 15 cl

Task 3
a 450 ml **b** 225 ml

Task 4
a 75 ml, 75 cl, 755 ml, 7.5 litres, 7505 ml, 7500 cl
b 47 ml, 410 ml, 4 litres, 4001 ml, 401 cl, 4.1 litres

Exploring Further...
1500 ml and 50 cl   1.2 litres and 80 cl
1 litre and 100 cl   60 cl and 1400 ml
200 ml and 1800 ml

Pages 28–29

Task 1
a £0.89 **b** £0.46 **c** £0.30 **d** £0.05
e £6.78 **f** £1.02

Task 2
a 590p **b** 809p **c** 436p **d** 1002p

Task 3
a 32p and 68p   **b** £3.15 and £1.85
74p and 26p   £3.40 and £1.60
42p and 58p   £2.15 and £2.85
23p and 77p   £4.49 and £0.51
87p and 13p   £4.40 and £0.60
36p and 64p

Task 4
a 73p **b** £1.18 **c** 91p **d** £1.90p

Exploring Further...
The cheapest option is Beechdale Woodland
Holidays: £980 + £250 = £1230

Pages 30–31

Task 1
a 5 past 6 in the morning   06:05
b quarter to 9 in the evening   20:45
c quarter past 3 in the afternoon 15:15
d 25 minutes to 2 in the afternoon 13:35
e 6 minutes to 8 in the morning   07:54

Task 2
a 23:43 **b** 11:21 **c** 08:13 **d** 18:57 **e** 13:25

Task 3
Paula, Philip and Patricia are all correct.

Task 4
a 420 minutes **b** 1800 seconds
c 108 months **d** 56 days

Exploring Further...
a 5 **b** 7 **c** 4

Pages 32–33

Task 1
a acute **b** acute **c** obtuse **d** right angle

Task 2
a acute **b** obtuse **c** obtuse
d right angle **e** acute **f** acute

Task 3
f, b, c, d, a, e

Exploring Further...
a unequal **b** unequal **c** equal **d** equal

Pages 34–35

Task 1
a An irregular shape **b** An equilateral triangle
c Two equal sides **d** A right-angled triangle

Task 2

	Two pairs of parallel sides	One pair of parallel sides	No parallel sides
4 right angles	square rectangle	×	×
2 acute and 2 obtuse angles	parallelogram rhombus	trapezium	kite

Exploring Further...

	3 sides	4 sides	More than 4 sides
2 pairs of equal sides	×	d, g, h,	×
2 equal sides only	f	×	×
All sides equal	a	e, i	j
No equal sides	c	b	k

Pages 36–37

Task 1
a Yes **b** Yes **c** No **d** No

Task 2
b and c